DIY DOG

100 Homemade Dog Toys, Treats, and Projects to Save You Time and Money

Mick Kremling

☐ **Copyright 2016 by Mick Kremling - All rights reserved.**

This document is geared towards providing exact and reliable information in regards to the topic and issue covered. The publication is sold with the idea that the publisher is not required to render accounting, officially permitted, or otherwise, qualified services. If advice is necessary, legal or professional, a practiced individual in the profession should be ordered.

- From a Declaration of Principles which was accepted and approved equally by a Committee of the American Bar Association and a Committee of Publishers and Associations.

In no way is it legal to reproduce, duplicate, or transmit any part of this document in either electronic means or in printed format. Recording of this publication is strictly prohibited and any storage of this document is not allowed unless with written permission from the publisher. All rights reserved.

The information provided herein is stated to be truthful and consistent, in that any liability, in terms of inattention or otherwise, by any usage or abuse of any policies, processes, or directions contained within is the solitary and utter responsibility of the recipient reader. Under no circumstances will any legal responsibility or blame be held against the publisher for any reparation, damages, or monetary loss due to the information herein, either directly or indirectly.

Respective authors own all copyrights not held by the publisher.

The information herein is offered for informational purposes solely, and is universal as so. The presentation of the information is without contract or any type of guarantee assurance.

The trademarks that are used are without any consent, and the publication of the trademark is without permission or backing by the trademark owner. All trademarks and brands within this book are for clarifying purposes only and are the owned by the owners themselves, not affiliated with this document.

DIY Homemade Dog Toys

Frozen Sock Chew Toy

What you need:

1. Two socks. The Longer, the better. (If you want to spice up the look of the toy, use some socks with cool designs on them.)
2. A sink or bucket of water
3. A freezer

Steps:

1. Take the two socks and tie them together in a balled up knot. (Tie 1st sock into a ball, this doesn't have to be perfect. Put 1st sock into the 2nd sock, tie a knot in the 2nd sock and peel back the remaining and wrap it around.)
2. Soak the socks generously in water.
3. Freeze it for about 1-3 hours.
4. Take that sucker out and give it to your pooch!

There you have it, the perfect, basically free, reusable chew toy for a hot summer day

DIY Ball Dog Toy

What you need:

1. A medium sized ball (old tennis balls or baseballs work great)
2. About half a yard of fabric (1.5 feet) (An old t-shirt or bandana will do)
3. A piece of ribbon (about a foot long)
4. A pair of scissors for cutting

Steps:

1. Cut the fabric into two strips, 6" x 14" works well, but you can use any size that works.
2. Placing the ball in the center of the fabric, fold the fabric in half and wrap it around the ball.
3. Grab your ribbon and tie it around the base of the ball, wrapping it around a couple times.
4. Cut the tail of the fabric into several 2 inch wide strips.
5. Now, using three strips at a time, braid them into sections, making the braids as tight as possible. (Your doggy will have a hard time ripping them apart!)

6. With the excess fabric at the end of your braid, tie knots to keep the braids in place.

Voila! Your buddy has a new, durable toy! Perfect for some tug of war!

The Crinkling Sock

What you need:

1. An empty plastic water bottle
2. A long sock

Steps:

1. Simply place an empty plastic water bottle inside the sock.
2. Using the open end of the sock, tie a good knot.

All done! You've made a simple, easy, durable toy for the dog that loves those crinkling noises.

This toy would cost you close to 10 bucks at the pet store, and we made it for under a dollar.

The Breakdown Boxer

(**Warning:** This one can get a bit messy! Prepare for a lot of box bits all over the floor)

What you need:

1. An empty cereal box (An egg carton works well too!)
2. Tape
3. Dog Treats

Steps:

1. Take an empty cereal box and be sure to remove any plastic bags from the inside.
2. Place a couple of your dog's treat of choice in the box.
3. Tape the box shut with some masking or duct tape.
4. Watch your dog tear it apart to get to his favorite goodies!

Now it's your turn, Dog broke it down, Human gets to clean up! A bit of a mess, but a whole lot of fun for your dog!

The Jar of Glory

What you need:

1. An empty plastic jar. (A Peanut butter jar works well)
2. Bacon Grease

Steps:

1. Swirl some bacon grease on the bottom of the jar.
2. Let the jar sit until the bacon grease is hardened.

Watch your dog keep himself busy for hours!

Bonus: Just give your dog an empty jar of peanut butter to clean out. You can then reuse that jar for the bacon grease.

Note: The ingredient Xylitol is used in some brands of peanut butter. It is harmless to humans but may be harmful and potentially fatal to your dog. PLEASE read the ingredients before giving peanut butter to your dog. Most commercial brands tend to be okay.

Treat Dispensing Tennis Ball

What you need:

1. Tennis ball, old or new.
2. Scissors or knife.
3. Your dog's favorite treats or biscuits

Steps:

1. Cut along or across the white "S" shape on the tennis ball about half way, so that it appears as a dispensable flap.
2. Insert dog treats and close flap.
3. Give it to your dog and let the fun commence!

Dog not interested in fetch? This is a great tool to use to help motivate your dog to fetch, just make sure the flap is sturdy enough to remain closed when you throw it.

Snack Sock

What you need:

1. Two somewhat thick socks.
2. Small dog treats

Steps:

1. Place dog treats inside one sock then ball it up (As you would when you put them in your sock drawer.)
2. Put that sock inside the empty sock and tie a knot to seal it inside.

Your dog will love the challenge of getting his favorite snacks out of the tightly wound sock puzzle.

Muffin Pan Ball Game

What you need:

1. A muffin pan (The more the better, preferably 12 hole)
2. Tennis balls, one for each hole.
3. Dog Treats

Steps:

1. Place a treat in each hole, however many you'd like.
2. Place a tennis ball on top of each.
3. Place the pan on the floor in front of your dog.
4. Watch your dog figure out one of the many ways to get to those treats!

You may have to reveal where the treats are the first couple of times you play with your dog, to get him interested. You can mix up the treats as you like, using tastier ones in harder to get spots. Just keep your pooch guessing and he'll never get tired of this fun game and neither will you.

Milk Jug o' Treats

What you need:

1. An empty milk jug
2. Medium sized treats. Large enough so they don't fall out of the jug easily.

Steps:

1. Remove the cap and any plastic rings from the top of the milk jug.
2. Place a dozen or so dog treats inside the jug.

Watch your dog bite, scratch and throw the jug around the house for hours trying to get those treats out.

The Toy Iceberg

What you need:

1. A Medium sized plastic bucket
2. A few dog toys
3. A Freezer

Steps:

1. Fill the bucket about half way with water.
2. Place any toys that sink in the bucket first, followed by the others.
3. Place the bucket in the freezer for 2-4 hours or overnight
4. Take the bucket it out, if you have difficulty getting the ice out, run some warm water over the bucket to help it loosen.

This big bucket of fun is perfect to keep your dog cool on a hot summer day. It will keep your dog busy for hours, as he tries to lick, bite, and free his favorite toys from their icy prison!

Bonus: Place some meaty treats in the water before you freeze it to give your doggy some incentive. (Make sure the treats are water proof, or they'll fall apart in the water.)

PVC Pipe Puzzle

What you need:

1. PVC pipe about 12 inches will do, but use however long you'd like.
2. Two PVC pipe end pieces
3. Dog kibble
4. A drill

Steps:

1. Drill some holes in random locations along your PVC pipe. Make sure these holes are just large enough for the kibble to fit through.
2. Put the two end pieces on either side of the pipe
3. Put a handful of dog kibble through the holes.

You're done! The great thing about this toy is that not only will it keep your dog busy for an hour or two, but you can always get more PVC pipe and go wild with your designs. Once a pipe gets too easy, you can increase the difficulty by drilling fewer holes or in harder spots, the possibilities are endless.

Toilet Paper Treat Tube

What you need:

1. A cardboard toilet paper or paper towel roll.
2. Dog Treats

Steps:

1. Grab a cardboard tube from the inside a toilet paper roll (or Paper Towel).
2. Fold one end of the tube together so that the opening is sealed off.
3. Put a few dog treats inside.
4. Fold the other end to completely seal off the tube so the treats will not fall out.

There you have it. Similar to the cereal box toy, expect a bit of a mess and a bunch of fun for your pup!

The Glove That Feeds

What you need:

1. An old cotton glove
2. Some small dog treats or kibble

Steps:

1. Place a few treats in each finger of the glove
2. Give it to your dog, kick back and relax!

Watch as your dog flings and tears his way to those treats.

Three T-shirt Braid Toy

What you need:

1. Three old T-shirts
2. Scissors

Steps:

1. Cut the T-shirts into strips vertically about 3-4 strips for each shirt, depending on how thick you want the toy.
2. Take all your strips and tie a knot at the top, so that the strips dangle down.
3. Start braiding in whichever way you prefer.
4. Near the end, tie another knot.

Though a little more complicated to make, this is a store quality, durable toy that even the roughest of chewers will have a tough time tearing,

Jar Puzzle

What you need:

1. A empty peanut butter jar
2. Three cardboard toilet paper rolls
3. Drill with wide bit
4. Small Dog Treats or Kibble

Steps:

1. Drill a hole on each side of the jar big enough for the treats or food to fit through.
2. Put 3 toilet paper rolls inside the jar.
3. Add the dog treats or kibble
4. Screw on the lid

Watch as your dog throws and rolls their new toy around, trying to get that food out. This puzzle teaches your dog to slow down their eating and figure out how to get the food out. Best of all, this toy normally goes for more than $30 retail! Talk about saving some money...

Sock Donuts

What you need:

1. Two medium/long socks (the thicker, the better)
2. Scissors

Steps:

1. Lay one sock over top of the other
2. Cut the top part off both socks
3. Turn them inside out
4. Slide one sock inside the other
5. Roll it all up
6. Fold the rest over the whole donut
7. Adjust how you want it to look

What better way to get your dog playing than a sock donut?! You can make tons of these, their durable, fun, and cost practically nothing to make. Spice up their look by adding your favorite designs with markers, or bits of cloth.

Bonus: Sneak a treat inside a donut to get your dog interested.

Refurbished Stuffed Animal

What you need:

1. A stuffed animal
2. A squeaker from an old dog toy
3. Scissors
4. Needle and thread

Steps:

1. Cut off any tags, plastic, or hard bits from the stuffed animal
2. Cut a hole just large enough to be able to fit the squeaker through
3. Push the squeaker so that it sit comfortable in the stuffing
4. Sew the opening closed, simple stitching will do, make sure it is tight as possible and finish by doubling knotting the thread

You can find all sorts of stuffed animals all over thrift stores or garage sales for less than a dollar. Also, depending on the size of the stuffed animal, you can always add more squeakers. Have a favorite hobby or interest but can't find it as a dog toy? Just make your own!

Sponge Toy for Older Dogs and Dogs with Sensitive Teeth

What you need:

1. A few dish sponges (not too firm)
2. A clean sock with no holes
3. (Optional) A squeaker or squeaky toy

Steps:

1. Insert the sponge all the way in the sock
2. Insert the squeaker into the sock if you have one
3. Tie a knot at the end of the sock

This is perfect for dogs that may have sensitive teeth or show little interest in toys due to chewing pain or lack of teeth.

Rolls and Bowl Boredom Buster

What you need:

- A medium bowl with a flat bottom (You can just use your dog's bowl)
- 6-10 Toilet paper rolls
- Kibble or treats

Steps:

1. Place as many toilet paper rolls as you can in the bowl, so they stand upright and sit snuggly
2. Place treats or kibble down the rolls
3. Watch as your figures out the best way to get to that food!

Ball and Rope

What you need:

1. Tennis ball
2. About 1-3 Feet of rope, depending on how big you want the toy
3. A Drill, or something to poke holes In the ball

Steps:

1. Drill two holes directly across from one another on the tennis ball
2. Slide the rope through both holes
3. Tie a knot on either end OR tie both ends together

This is a very inexpensive, flexible toy that's durable and takes very little time to make. Great for tug of war!

The Rattlesnake

What you need:

1. A Prescription pill bottle, with child proof lid
2. Some dry uncooked beans or something equivalent
3. A few socks

Steps:

1. Put about ten or so beans in the prescription bottle and close the lid. You want a nice loud "rattle" sound.
2. Ball a sock up and push it down into another sock.
3. Push the pill bottle down the sock also
4. Push another sock into the first sock to keep the pill bottle snug and in place.
5. Tie a knot on top of the sock and you're done!

This is a great toy to kick start your dog's curiosity. I like to take a marker and draw some eyes and voila, a snake!

Hose n Stick

What you need:

1. 1 small stick or branch
2. 1 piece of old garden hose

Steps:

1. Put a 3 inch long piece of stick, and put it in one end of the garden hose piece.
2. Make sure it fits very snug
3. Curve the hose around and put the open end over the expose piece of stick

DIY Dog Treats

Baked Bacon Bars

What you need:

- 1 ½ cups whole wheat flour
- ½ cup wheat germ
- ½ cup melted bacon fat
- 1 Large Egg
- ½ cup cold water

Steps:

1. Preheat oven to 350 degrees F
2. Combine all ingredients in a bowl and mix by until dough forms. If the dough is too sticky, add more flour. Add more bacon fat or water if dough is too firm.
3. Roll dough out flat to a thickness of a little less than ½ an inch.
4. Cut dough in 1x4 inch bars, transfer to a cookie sheet and poke a few divots into each bar (I like to use a fork).
5. Bake for 20 minutes or until slightly brown

6. Turn off oven, flip bars over, place back in oven to cool down and crisp up.

Apple-Cheese Biscuits

What you need:

- 2 cups barley flour
- 1/2 cup old fashioned oats
- 1/3 shredded cheddar cheese
- 1/4 cup grated Parmesan cheese
- 1/3 cup unsweetened apple sauce
- 2 tbsp. olive oil
- 3 tbsp. water

Steps:

1. Preheat oven to 350 degrees F
2. Line a baking sheet with non-stick parchment paper, set aside
3. Mix all ingredients in a large bowl to form dough
4. Roll dough out flat about 1/4 inch thick
5. Use your favorite cookie cutter to cut out shapes about 3 inch long
6. Space biscuits out on baking sheet about an inch apart

7. Bake for about 30 minutes or until golden brown

8. Turn off oven and let treats cool until firm. (You can also put them in a refrigerator)

Homemade Puppucino (Caffeine Free)

What you need:

- 2 tsp. vanilla extract
- 2 tbsp. coconut sugar
- 14 oz. coconut cream, refrigerated

Steps:

1. Take coconut cream from fridge, remove top of can and spoon out the thick layer of coconut cream that should have separated on the top. Transfer it to a chilled mixing bowl. Don't use any water from the cream.
2. Whisky coconut cream for 4 minutes or until the cream becomes light and fluffy.
3. Add in your sweetener and vanilla and beat.
4. Serve!

Avoid light coconut milk or brands that are made with guar gum.

Dog Beer (Non-Alcoholic)

What you need:

- 1 cup chicken or beef stock
- 2 tbsp. frozen spinach, chopped

Steps:

1. Pour stock into a pint size jar such as a mason jar
2. Chop up spinach and add to the jar.
3. Let sit in refrigerator for 24 hours, shake occasionally
4. Strain the spinach and pour into an old clean beer bottle.
5. Have a cold one with your new drinking buddy!

Peanut Butter Banana Frozen Treats

What you need:

- Two 12 slot ice club trays
- 2 tbsp. honey
- 2 heaping tbsp. peanut butter
- 32 oz. plain nonfat yogurt
- 1 banana
- A blender

Steps:

1. Add all ingredient s into a blender and blend well
2. Pour mixture into ice cube trays
3. Put in freezer for 4-6 hours
   (Run warm water over the bottom of the tray if treats are difficult to remove after freezing)

Breakfast Bonanza

What you need:

- 3 eggs
- 3 cups cooked rice or quinoa
- 12 slices turkey bacon
- 1 cup unsweetened applesauce

Steps:

1. Cook and crumble bacon into tiny pieces
2. Cook rice or quinoa until fluffy
3. Scramble eggs
4. Mix all ingredients together with applesauce and serve!

Frozen Chicken Broth Milk Bones

What you need:

- Ice cube trays
- Milk Bones
- Chicken broth

Steps:

1. Pour chicken broth into ice cube tray
2. Lay milk bone in each hole (The small bones will fit, if you only have large bones, just break them in half)
3. Put in freezer for 4-6 hours or until frozen

Sweet Potato Jerky

What you need:

- Fresh, large sweet potatoes (number will depend on how much strips you make)

Steps:

1. Preheat the oven to 225 degrees F
2. Scrub potatoes; make sure there is no mold on skins.
3. Cut the sweet potatoes lengthwise into ½ to 2/3 inch strips
4. Place them on a non-stick baking pan
5. Bake the strips for 3-4 hours, longer if you'd like them crunchy
6. Let strips cool before storing in an airtight container

Puppy Punch-sicles

What you need:

- 2 bananas
- 2 cups blueberries, frozen
- ½ tsp. cinnamon
- 1 cup decaf green tea
- 14 oz. can coconut milk

Steps:

1. Brew the tea (make sure it's decaf, caffeine is toxic to dogs). Let set in the refrigerator until cool.
2. Place other ingredients in a blender and puree
3. Stir in the tea
4. Serve as a drink or freeze in ice cube trays

Frozen Apple Yogurt Delights

What you need:

- Ice cube tray
- ½ cup unsweetened apple sauce
- ½ cup chopped apple
- 1 cup non-fat yogurt

Steps:

1. Mix all ingredients together in a bowl
2. Spoon out mixture into ice cube tray
3. Freeze 4-6 hours or until hard

Homemade Pill Pockets for Dogs

What you need: (Makes about 30)

- 1 cup flour
- ½ cup crunchy peanut butter
- ½ cup milk

Steps:

1. Mix all ingredients together in a mixing bowl
2. Take a medium pinch of mix, and form into a ball
3. Poke a small hole in each using the tip of your finger
4. Pop a pill in and seal off opening
5. Store in refrigerator or freezer

Fish Cakes

What you need:

- 1 large egg
- 2 cups mashed potatoes
- 15oz can of salmon or tuna
- 1 cup plain bread crumbs
- 1 tsp. lemon juice
- 1 tsp. drill seed
- 1 tbsp. parsley
- ½ tsp. sea salt

Steps:

1. Drain fish and remove any bone
2. In a bowl, mix all ingredients well
3. Form into ½ inch thick patties about 3 inches wide
4. Place patties on non-stick baking sheet
5. Bake at 350 degrees F for 10 minutes, flip patties over, baking another 15 minutes until slightly brown.
6. Remove from oven and let cool 5 minutes
7. Store in airtight container for up to 5 days

Cheese and Bacon Bites

What you need:

- ¾ cup white flour
- ¾ cup whole wheat flour
- ½ teas baking soda
- ½ cup vegetable oil
- 2/3 cup loose brown sugar
- 2 large eggs
- 1 teas vanilla extract
- 2/3 cup quick oat
- ¾ cup shredded cheddar cheese
- ½ cup real bacon bits

Steps:

1. In a bowl combine both flours with baking soda
2. In a separate bowl, mix together oil, vanilla, eggs, and brown sugar
3. Add flour mixture and blend well
4. Stir in oats, cheese and bacon bits
5. Drop tbsp. sized bites onto a cookie sheet
6. Bake at 350 degrees for 15 minutes

Puppermint Patties

What you need:

- 3 cups oat flour
- ¼ cup dry milk
- ½ cup chicken stock
- 1 egg
- 2 tbsp. fresh mint
- 1 tsp. baking powder
- ¼ cup fresh parsley

Steps:

1. Finely chop parsley and mint.
2. Mix all together all ingredients until dough is formed
3. Roll dough out to ¼ inch on lightly floured surface, use your favorite cookie cutter or a jar lid
4. Place patties on non-stick baking sheet
5. Bake at 350 degrees F for 30 minutes
6. Let cool and serve

Quick n Easy Meat Strips

What you need:

- 2 jars baby food meat
- ¼ cup whole wheat flour
- ¼ cup white flour
- ¼ cup parmesan cheese

Steps:

1. Mix all ingredients together
2. Dump whole batch onto the middle of a greased cookie pan
3. With slightly floured hands, press it flat until about ¼ inch thick
4. With a floured knife, cut into strips
5. Bake at 350 degrees for 20 minutes
6. Store in refrigerator

Peanut Butter Cookies

What you need:

- ¾ cup white flour
- ¼ cup powdered milk
- 1 egg
- ¼ cup vegetable oil
- ½ tsp. vanilla
- 1 spoonful peanut butter
- 1 tbsp. honey
- 1 tsp. baking soda

Steps:

1. Mix all ingredients together into a thin batter
2. By teaspoonful, drop batter onto a greased baking pan and bake 7-10 minutes at 325 degrees or until golden brown
3. Watch carefully, due to their thinness, they cook quickly

Quick n Easy Crunchy Oatmeal Treats

What you need:

- 1 cup water
- ½ cup whole wheat flour
- 1 tsp. baking soda
- 3 cups quick oats
- 2 eggs

Steps:

1. Mix all ingredients in a bowl and drop by teaspoonful onto a baking pan
2. Slightly flatten the treats with a fork
3. Bake at 350 degrees for 12-15 minutes
4. Makes about 50 treats

Chicken n Rice Bites

What you need:

- 1 cup chicken, diced or shredded
- 1 cup brown or wild rice
- 1 egg, beaten
- 1 tbsp. parsley, diced
- 3 tbsp. rice flour

Steps:

1. Preheat oven to 350 degrees F
2. Combine all ingredients in a mixing bowl and stir until mixed well
3. Using a spoon, pack mixture onto baking sheet, about an inch apart
4. Bake for 25 minutes or until top turns golden brown
5. Let cool. Serve or store in refrigerator, good for about 5 days

Peanut Butter Bones

What you need:

- ½ cup skim milk
- ½ cup peanut butter
- ½ tbsp. baking powder
- 1 cup whole wheat flour

Steps:

1. Preheat oven to 375 degrees F
2. Grease baking pan or use parchment paper
3. In a bowl mix together milk and peanut butter until smooth
4. Stir in flour and baking powder until blended well
5. Roll dough onto a lightly floured surface until about ¼ inch thick
6. Cut into your favorite cookie cutter shapes and place 2 inches apart onto baking sheet
7. Bake for 20 minutes until slightly brown
8. Let cool and serve!

Fruity Oatmeal Bites

What you need:

- 1 cup oats
- 1 banana, ripe
- 1 cup shredded carrot
- 1.5 cups whole wheat flour
- ¼ cup unsweetened apple sauce
- 1/8 cup water

Steps:

1. Preheat oven to 350 F
2. Mash the carrots with the banana, and add apple sauce and water
3. Add in oats and gradually add flour until dough is formed
4. Lightly flour a surface and roll dough to about ½ inch thick
5. Use a small cookie cutter and place cut out treats on a non-stick baking sheet
6. Bake for 25 minutes and then turn off oven, let bites sit inside for an additional 2-3 hours, creating a chewy or crunchy texture.

Carrot Apple Treats

What you need:

- 1 cup grated carrots
- 1 cup whole wheat flour
- 1 egg
- ½ cup unsweetened apple sauce

Steps:

1. Preheat oven to 350 degrees F
2. Mix all ingredients until dough forms
3. Roll dough into small balls and place on a non-stick baking sheet
4. Press pieces so that they are about ¼ an inch thick
5. Bake until golden brown and let cool

Bonus: Add ½ tsp. of salt to increase shelf life

Chicken Jerky Strips

What you need:

- 2-4 boneless chicken breast

Steps:

1. Preheat oven to 200 degrees F
2. Remove any excess fat, turn the chicken breast on its side and using a paring knife, slice breast into 1/8 inch thick strips
3. Set strips on a baking sheet and bake for 2 hours
4. Check chicken before removing, you want it dry and hard
5. Allow jerky to cool completely before serving
6. Store extra chicken in fridge, lasts up to two weeks

Kibble Treats

What you need:

- 2 cups dry dog food
- Blender
- Water

Steps:

1. In the blender, add 2 cups of dry dog food and grind into a powder
2. Pour powder into a mixing bowl and sad about 1 to 1 ½ cups of water, stirring until a dough is formed
3. Shape dough into small cookie shapes, flattening slightly with a spoon
4. Put treats on an ungreased baking sheet and bake at 350 degrees for 30 minutes or until crispy
5. Let cool then serve!
6. Treats may be stored safely in refrigerator for up to 7 days.

Canned Dog Food Treats

What you need:

- 1 can wet dog food
- Microwave
- Knife

Steps:

1. Shake loaf of wet food out of can and cut into ¼ thick slices then cut into bite sized pieces
2. Bake the treats in microwave on high for 3 minutes
3. Let cool then serve
4. Store treats in refrigerator for up to 7 days

Peanut Butter Banana Crunchy Treats

What you need:

- 3 Cups old fashioned Oats
- 2 Ripe Bananas, mashed
- ¼ cup Peanut Butter
- ¼ cup coconut oil

Steps:

1. Preheat oven to 350 Degrees F
2. Mix all ingredients together in a large bowl until dough is formed and no longer sticks
3. On a lightly floured surface, knead dough 3-5 times and roll to about ¼ inch thick
4. Take your preferred cookie cutter and cut desired shapes, place on non-stick baking sheet
5. Bake for 10-14 minutes until edges are golden brown
6. Let cool and serve!

Flea Prevention Dog Treats

What you need:

- 1 1/8 cups organic coconut oil
- ½ cup Brewer's yeast, slightly rounded
- 2 small ice cube trays

Steps:

1. Combine melted coconut oil and yeast together in a blender, blend until smooth
2. Carefully pour mixture into ice cube trays
3. Let sit in freezer until solid
4. Serve!

Bacon Sticks

What you need:

- ¼ cup crumbled bacon or bacon bits
- 1 egg
- 1 ¼ cup milk
- 1 tbsp. honey
- 4 tbsp. bacon fat
- 3 cups Oat flour

Steps:

1. Preheat oven to 350 degrees F
2. In a large mixing bowl, whisk together milk, egg, honey, bacon fat, and bacon
3. Stir in the flour ½ a cup at a time until dough is formed
4. Knead the dough until fully combined
5. Roll dough out onto lightly floured surface into a rectangle measuring 4 inch by 12 inch
6. Cut out 4 inch by ½ inch sticks
7. Line the sticks on a non-stick baking pan and bake for 30 minutes
8. Let cool before serving

9. Store in refrigerator up to 7 days

Homemade Doggy Breath Mints

What you need:

- 2 ½ cups old fashioned oats
- ½ cup fresh mint, finely chopped
- ½ cup fresh parsley, finely chopped
- 1 large egg
- ¼ cup of water
- 3 tbsp. coconut oil

Steps:

1. Preheat oven to 325 degrees F
2. Add oats to blender and pulse until a flour like consistency
3. In a large mixing bowl, whisk together parsley, mint, egg, water, and oil. Add oats powder and stir.
4. Knead dough a couple of times onto a lightly floured surface
5. Flatten dough to about 1/8" thick
6. Using a cookie cutter or knife cut about 40 mints and place ¼ inch apart on a non-stick baking sheet

7. Bake 35-40 minutes or until golden and crisp
8. Allow mints to cool then serve and store in air tight container

Hypoallergenic Oatmeal Almond Dog Treats

What you need:

- 1 Cup Rice Flour
- ½ Cup Almond Butter
- ½ Cup Oatmeal
- 2 Eggs
- 2 Tbsp. Water

Steps:

1. Preheat oven to 350 Degrees
2. In a mixing bowl, combine all ingredients except water, mix thoroughly.
3. Add water gradually until a dough forms
4. Roll dough to ¼ inch thickness on a slightly floured surface
5. Cut into desired shapes
6. Bake for 10-12 minutes until slightly browned
7. Let cool, store in airtight container

Treats for Diabetic Dogs

What you need:

- ½ cup whole wheat flour
- 2 eggs
- 1 ½ lbs. beef liver, cut into pieces
- Food processor

Steps:

1. Preheat oven to 350 degrees F
2. Place the liver into food processor, pulse until finely chopped. (If you have room, add eggs and flour also otherwise transfer to a bowl and stir in flour and eggs).
3. Spread mixture evenly on a non-stick baking sheet
4. Bake for 15 minutes until firm in center.
5. Let cool and cut into squares
6. Store in sealed container in refrigerator

Frozen Apple Delights

What you need:

- Two Apples of your preference
- 1 cup nonfat plain Greek yogurt
- Water
- Blender
- Ice cube tray

Steps:

1. Slice 2 apples into small pieces, remove seeds and core
2. Mix apple slices, yogurt, and a splash of water in a blender, and liquefy
3. Pour mixture into an ice cube tray and freeze for 3-5 hours or until hard

Homemade Pupperoni

What you need:

- 1 cup oat flour
- 1 ¾ cup rye flour
- ½ cup pepperoni shredded
- ½ cup Romano cheese, shredded
- 6 oz. can tomato paste
- ¼ tsp. oregano
- ¼ tsp. parsley
- 1 egg
- ¼ cup water

Steps:

1. Mix all ingredients in a large bowl
2. Roll out to ¼ inch thick and cut with a pizza cutter or cookie cutter
3. Place on a non-stick baking sheet
4. Bake at 350 degrees F for up to 15 minutes or until golden brown
5. Let cool and serve. Store up to a week in refrigerator

Cheese Crackers

What you need:

- 1 cup whole wheat flour
- 1 cup shredded cheddar cheese
- 1 tsp. brewer's yeast
- 1 tbsp. unsalted butter, soft
- ½ cup evaporated milk

Steps:

1. Mix flour and cheese together in a bowl
2. Add butter then slowly add milk while mixing, until dough is formed.
3. Knead dough 3-5 times
4. Roll out thinly on parchment paper
5. Slice small squares using a pizza cutter
6. Move paper to a baking sheet
7. Bake at 300 degrees for 15 minutes then turn over and bake for another 10 until crispy and lightly browned
8. Turn off oven and let sit in oven for an hour with door open slightly

Almond Banana Puppy Treats

What you need:

- 1 egg
- 1/3 ripe banana
- ¾ cup unsalted almond butter
- 1 tsp. ground cinnamon

Steps:

1. Preheat oven to 350 degrees F
2. Using a fork, mash banana in a mixing bowl then add all other ingredients and mix well
3. Spoon out coin sized dollops onto a non-stick baking pan and bake for 5 minutes
4. After 5 minutes, turn pan and bake for another 5 minutes
5. Remove from oven and let cool
6. Lasts 5-7 days

Holiday Ginger Snap Teats

What you need:

- 2 cups almond flour
- 1/2-3/4 cup peanut butter
- ½ cup coconut flour
- 3 tbs. ground ginger
- 1 tbs. cinnamon
- ¼ cup water

Steps:

1. Preheat oven to 320 degrees F
2. Mix all ingredients together in a mixing bowl and form a ball with dough
3. Roll dough flat on a slightly floured surface and using a cookie cutter cut out the individual treats. If you don't have a cookie cutter I like to use a jar lid, get creative!
4. Place treats onto non-stick baking pan
5. Bake for 25 minutes
6. Turn oven off and leave treats in the oven for 45 more minutes until treats are crisp
7. Serve!

No Bake Peanut Butter Pumpkin Balls

What you need:

- 1 cup pumpkin puree
- ¼ cup peanut butter
- ¼ cup milk
- 3 cups old fashioned oats, divided
- Electric mixer for convenience

Steps:

1. Beat pumpkin puree, peanut butter and milk in a mixing bowl until well combined, about 2-3 minutes
2. Gradually add 2 ½ cups oats, continue beating
3. Using a small scoop, roll mixture in 1 ½ inch balls, forming about 20.
4. Coat balls in remaining ½ cup of oats
5. Cover and place in refrigerator until firm)about an hour)

Tuna Treats

What you need:

- Two 6oz. cans tuna (do not drain)
- 1 ½ cup whole wheat flour
- 1 tbsp. garlic powder
- 2 eggs, lightly beaten

Steps:

1. Mix all ingredients together in a mixing bowl
2. Spread mixture out to about an inch thick on a non-stick baking sheet
3. Bake in oven at 350 degrees for about 20 minutes

Turkey Pumpkin Gummy Snacks

What you need:

- Ice cube trays
- ½ cup cooked turkey
- ½ cup pumpkin puree
- 1 tbsp. molasses
- 1 tsp. cinnamon
- ¼ cup water
- 2 packs unflavored gelatin
- 2 cups boiling water
- Blender

Steps:

- Puree all ingredients except gelatin and boiling water in a blender until smooth
- Pour into a large bowl and sprinkle 2 packets of gelatin in and let stand 1 minute
- Pour boiling water over the puree and gelatin then mix well
- Pour into ice trays and refrigerate about 6 hours

Frozen Watermelon Delights

What you need:

- 2 cups Seedless Watermelon
- 1 cup Coconut milk or coconut water
- ¼ cup Honey
- Blender
- Ice cube trays

Steps:

1. Put all three ingredients in a blender and puree until very liquid, like juice.
2. Pour the mixture into ice cube tray
3. Place in freezer for about an hour
4. Enjoy this refreshing summer treat! (You can eat them too!)

Cheesy Treats

What you need:

- 4 cups flour
- ½ cup vegetable oil
- 1 cup shredded cheese of your choice, I prefer cheddar (and so does my dog!)
- 1 egg
- 1 cup milk

Steps:

1. Mix all ingredients together and then knead mixture on a floured surface a few times
2. Roll out mixture to ¼ inch thick on a non-stick baking pan
3. Cut treats into small squares
4. Bake for 25 minutes at 400 degrees F
5. Let cool and serve

Baby Food Dog Treats

What you need:

- 2 cups whole wheat flour
- Two 4 oz. jars of baby food (make sure it does not contain onions, grapes or raisins)

Steps:

1. Preheat oven to 350 degrees F
2. Mix ingredients together into a firm dough
3. Roll dough to 1.4 inch thick
4. Cut out preferred shapes with cookie cutter
5. Place treats on non-stick baking pan about an inch apart
6. Bake 20-25 minutes
7. Let cool and store in air tight container

PB and Beef Cookies

What you need:

- 1 egg
- ½ cup beef broth
- ½ cup peanut butter
- 2 ½ cup flour
- 2 tbsp. brown sugar
- 1 tbsp. butter

Steps:

1. Preheat oven to 350 degrees F
2. Combine all dry ingredients in a mixing bowl
3. Add in butter and peanut butter
4. Mix in eggs and beef broth
5. Roll a small handful of dough into your hand and create desired cookie shape
6. Place dough on non-stick baking sheet
7. Bake for 25 minutes or until crunchy

Peanut Butter and Fruit Ice Ring

What you need:

- 2 tbsp. Flax Seeds
- ½ cup peanut butter
- 1 cup chopped strawberries
- Bundt cake pan
- Water

Steps:

1. Blend the peanut butter and water, then pour into Bundt pan
2. Add fruit and flax seeds
3. Freeze for 4-6 hours
4. Give to your pup outside, it can get quite messy!

Sweet Potato Cookies

What you need:

- 1 large sweet potato
- ¼ cup applesauce unsweetened
- 1/8 cup honey
- 1 egg
- 1 cup whole wheat flour

Steps:

1. Preheat oven to 350 degrees F
2. Peel and cut sweet potato into inch sized chunks.
3. Place the potato pieces into a microwave safe bowl, cover with napkin and heat for 2 minutes or until soft
4. Mash potato chunks with fork
5. Lightly beat egg and stir into potato mixture
6. Gradually stir in flour until thoroughly combined
7. Scoop mixture into 1 inch mounds on non-stick baking sheet
8. Bake for 20 minutes

9. Let cool before serving

Minty Pineapple Cucumber Pupsicles

What you need:

- 2 cups grated cucumber
- 2 cups pureed pineapple
- 4 chopped mint leaves
- Popsicle molds or ice cube trays
- Optional: Bullysticks or any stick shaped treats

Steps:

1. Mix all ingredients together in a bowl until smooth
2. Pour mixture into popsicle mold or ice cube tray (You can use rod shaped treats for a popsicle stick)
3. Put in freezer let sit for about 6 hours or until frozen
4. Run warm water over mold to help loosen popsicles

Birthday Cake for Dogs

What you need:

- 2 ½ cups water
- ½ cup canned pumpkin
- 1 egg slightly beaten
- ½ tsp. vanilla extract
- ¼ cup peanut butter
- 3 ½ cups whole wheat flour
- ½ cup oats
- 1 tbsp. baking powder
- ½ tsp. cinnamon

Steps:

1. Preheat oven to 350 degrees F
2. In a medium mixing bowl, mix water, egg, pumpkin, vanilla and peanut butter.
3. In a large bowl, combine oats, flour, baking powder and cinnamon
4. Mix dry and wet ingredients together and stir well.
5. Spoon into a greased 6 inch pan until 2/3 full
6. Bake for 35-40 minutes or until firm

7. Let cool and store in an open container in the refrigerator.

8. Give to your dog in small doses

Birthday Cake Icing for Dogs

What you need:

- 4 ounces plain yogurt
- 2-4 ounces of peanut butter

Steps:

1. Whisk both ingredients together in a bowl.
2. If your frosting is too thick, you can thin it out with canola oil.
3. If too thin, gradually add some cornstarch or flour to thicken
4. Frost away!

Foods to Avoid

With all these delicious recipes it's always encouraged and recommended to change up some ingredients for sake of convenience and to cater to your dog's needs or preference. In selecting substitutes we must all be aware of the certain foods and chemicals that can be dangerous, even fatal, to your beloved friend.

Here's a comprehensive list of foods to avoid giving your dog, as found on the official ASPCA website:

- Onions
- Garlic
- Avocados
- Peaches
- Sugar
- Chocolate in any form
- Tea
- Coffee beans
- Yeast dough
- Salt
- Grapes and raisins

- Tomato leaves and stems
- Potato leaves and stems
- Rhubarb leaves
- Mold or spoiled foods
- Alcohol
- Xylitol (found is some brands of nut butter)
- Some mushrooms
- Walnuts and Macadamia Nuts

Remember, all of these treats listed in this book are intended to be used in moderation. These recipes are not a substitute for a quality dog food.

DIY Projects, Tips and Tricks

Homemade Dog Shampoo

What you need:

- 1 cup organic apple cider vinegar
- 2 tbsp. lemon dish detergent
- 2 tbsp. pure Aloe Vera
- An empty bottle to store shampoo

Steps:

1. Mix 1 cup organic apple cider vinegar with 2 tbsp. lemon dish detergent
2. Add 2 tbsp. pure Aloe Vera
3. Shake bottle well

DIY Cooling Bed

What you need:

- Two old towels
- Pin and needle with thread
- Zip lock Baggies
- Frozen Peas

Steps:

1. Take your two towels and lay them on top of one another, lining up the edges
2. Stich 3 of the sides closed using a whip stitch
3. Stitch the last side, leaving the middle partly unstitched, in order to place the cooling packs inside
4. Grab 4-6 bags of zip locked frozen peas
5. Be sure to supervise and ensure your dog does not try to get at the peas

Homemade Flea Shampoo

What you need:

- ¼ cup Castile Soap
- ½ cup Apple Cider Vinegar
- 1 cup hot water
- Lice Comb
- Squirt Bottle
- Bath tub

Steps:

1. Run a bath of slightly warm water for your dog
2. Mix all ingredients into the squirt bottle and shake well
3. Apply from the top of your dog's head all the way to the end of their tail, scrubbing it in well
4. Let sit for 5 minutes
5. Using the lice comb, comb fleas off your dog into the water.
6. Rinse several times very well
7. Dry your dog with a tower
8. You may need to repeat this for several days

Chalkboard Food/Water Bowls

What you need:

- A ceramic bowl (Size depending on your dog)
- Frog tape
- Chalkboard Spray-paint

Steps:

1. Using the tape, cover the portions of the bowl you do not want to get paint on.
2. With even coats, spray your bowl with the chalkboard paint.
3. Let dry for a few hours
4. Grab some chalk and have some fun!

Broth for Upset Stomachs

What you need:

- 1 chicken leg OR beef bone with some meat still attached
- ½ tbsp. finely chopped sage
- ½ tbsp. finely chopped basil
- ½ tbsp. finely chopped rosemary

Steps:

1. Put chicken/beef in pot of water on stove
2. Add herbs
3. Simmer on a low/medium-low heat until meat is cooked
4. Remove meat from pot, leave herbs and fat in water
5. Store broth in a glass container/jar in refrigerator
6. You can either leave the excess meat in the broth(without the bone) or eat/give it to your dog for a treat
7. Add broth to your dog's food during meal time

8. Give about ½ a cup to large dogs, ¼ a cup for medium and 1/8 for small dogs

Rubber Glove Hair Remover

Don't have a lint roller? Don't want to pay almost five bucks for one (adds up overtime)?

A simple rubber glove will have the same effect. You can pick one up for less than a dollar at most stores, and it lasts forever!

Trouble Brushing Teeth

Some dogs just don't respond well to us going near their teeth, especially with a toothbrush!

If you're having trouble brushing your dog's teeth try spreading the toothpaste on your dog's favorite chew toy. Eventually your dog will get accustomed to that tasty paste and may let you brush their teeth the old fashioned way. Once done though, you should immediately reward your pup, until they become completely comfortable with it.

Bad Breath Fix

If you're dog suffers from bad breath skip the expensive breath treats and do this simple trick.

Grab some fresh parsley and chop it up. Sprinkle a handful on your dog's food and a bit in their water bowl. Over the course of a week or two, if you're consistent, you should notice a significant improvement in freshness!

Trouble Walking Multiple Dogs at Once

Have a few dogs and a sore hand? It can be a real pain (literally) to have multiple leashes in your hand, especially if your dogs are pullers.

The remedy is a Giant Carabineer! You can pick one up for less than five bucks at any hardware store. Trust me on this, you won't regret it. Walks for me and my boys have become a MUCH more pleasant experience.

Dog Bed Cover

Having trouble washing your dog's bed? Save hours of frustrating clean by simply covering the bed with an old pillow case. As dirt and hair add up just slip the pillow case off and wash.

Dogs with Mats

If your dog gets mats in their hair often a simple trick is to just sprinkle some baby powder on them. The powder will help loosen the mats so you easily brush them out.

Oh, and your dog will also smell nice, a welcomed bonus!

For Quick Eaters

Does your dog "wolf" down his food? Ingesting too much food too fast can lead to choking, gagging, and in some cases digestive problems.

An easy way to curb this behavior is to put a tennis ball in their bowl with their food. Your dog will be forced to slow down and move the ball around to get to the food.

Dog Scared of Thunderstorms and Bad Weather

If your dog gets nervous and skittish during storms, this may help.

During a storm, run a dryer sheet over your dog's fur. Most of the time it's not the actual storm that scares them, it's the static electricity built up in their fur.

Pet Hair Remover

Have a heavy shedder and no time or energy to vacuum?

Grab a squeegee! Run it across carpet, furniture, clothes, you name it. The squeegee easily rakes up all the hair, making it no hassle to clean up.

Chapping and Cracking Paws

It's all too common for dog's to suffer from cracking paws, especially during winter.

An easy way to prevent this is to apply a bit of Vaseline to each paw before you take your dog on a walk.

Afterwards, gently rinse their paws in warm water to get rid of any salt or chemicals that may have latched on. Cracking and chapping paws can be a very painful experience for your pooch, so do them this favor. Remember they don't have the luxury of boots like us!

Hydrogen Peroxide

If your dog gets into something poisonous such as chocolate, raisins, grapes, etc. Giving them hydrogen peroxide will induce vomiting, potentially saving your dog's life if done quickly. Give 1 teaspoon per 5 pounds of body weight. Always take your dog to the vet regardless if it was successful, to be absolutely sure your pooch is safe.

Emergency List and First Aid

There are multiple print-ready lists available on the web where you can fill in all of your pet's emergency contact numbers. There are also picture guides on how to perform CPR, artificial respiration and Heimlich maneuver. You can also find inexpensive first aid kits at your local pet store that should include this information as well as key medical supplies for you pup.

I recommended printing these off and becoming familiar with each one. Then place them in an easy to find spot that you'll remember such as on the refrigerator or by your dog's food area.

The difference between having ready access and knowledge of these in emergency situations can be lifesaving. Be prepared today so you are not unprepared tomorrow.

Skunk Spray

So doggy got a bit too close to the wrong end of a skunk, eh?

Here's a simple concoction to rid yourself and your pooch of the stink/

Mix a bottle of hydrogen peroxide ¼ a cup of baking soda and 2 teaspoons of liquid soap.

Whilst giving your dog a bath, thoroughly wash and rinse him with the mixture and warm water. The final product will do wonders in getting rid of that hard to rid smell and you won't be spending tons of money on expensive specialty soap, which is basically the same ingredient!

DIY Dog Poop Bag Dispenser

What you need:

- Small plastic container with lid (such as an empty prescription container)
- A carabineer
- Zip tie
- Dog poop bags
- Electric drill

Steps:

1. Drill 2 small holes in the lid of a plastic bottle. Large enough for the zip tie to fit through and far enough apart for a carabineer to get tied on,
2. Use the drill to make a straight line along the side of the bottle so that the bags can be easily pulled out.
3. Insert a roll of poop bags into the container
4. Place the carabineer onto the lid with a zip tie
5. Cut off any excess part of the zip tie
6. Put lid onto container
7. Decorate as you wish

8. Just clip the carabineer to your belt or dog's leash and you're good to go!

Senior Dogs and Dogs with Sensitive Teeth

If you own a senior dog, eventually they may start to suffer from tooth decay and gum pain, which can hinder their ability to eat dry food.

By simply adding a bit of water to their dry food and placing it in the microwave for about 20 seconds can soften their food enough to ease any pain your dog may have during chow time.

Digging Dog

Have problems with your dog digging up your yard? Is Fido trying to escape his way under the fence, or helping with gardening?

Stop your dog destroying your yard by introducing a sandbox to fill his digging desires. You can bury some of their favorite toys or some treats to encourage your dog to dig up the sand instead of the flowers.

You can save money and personalize your sandbox by building it yourself. A simple Google search will reveal hundreds of pet parent approved designs.

Homemade Elizabethan Collar/ Cone

What you need:

- A plastic flower pot appropriate for your dog's size (An ice cream bucket can work too)
- A tape measure
- Box cutter/sharp knifes/scissors
- 2 threads of twine, about 2-3 feet in length

Steps:

1. Measure the area from ½ an inch in front of your dog's nose to the collar on its neck. This will be the length of the cone.
2. Loosen your dog's normal collar and slip it off without unfastening it and measure the circumference, this will be the circumference of the neck hole for the cone.
3. Draw a hole in the bottom of the container that is slightly larger than the circumference of the dog's collar.
4. Cut out the hole with a knife/box cutter
5. Cover the edges of the hole with masking tape. This will make the cone more comfortable

6. Poke small holes around the open about ½ an inch from the cut edge with a pair of scissors
7. Thread a piece of twine through these holes, leaving the ends dangling for now
8. Place the cone over the dog's head and pull at it slightly to ensure that it will not slip off
9. Place your dog's original collar back onto the dog and attach it to the cone with the twine

Clothes/Costumes for Small Dogs

Love dressing your little friend in all sorts of costumes and cute clothes? Save the expensive trips to the pet store!

An easy way to find new get ups for your dog is to use doll clothes. Too old to play with that old doll? Give her clothes to your pup instead! Last minute Halloween costume? We got you covered!

Pee Stains

Skip the expensive pet store cleaning products and use this instead.

Take a bit of baking soda and cover the wet spot. Let it dry for a few minutes then vacuum over it. The smell and stain will be gone forever!

NOTE: Baking soda can be toxic to dogs, make sure your dog stays away from the spot while you're cleaning it.

Trouble with Pulling During Walks

If you have trouble keeping your dog by your side on walks, try this.

First of all, pick a side you want your dog to walk on, either left or right side of you and stick to that side every walk.

Next hold your leash in the hand opposite the side you dog walks. If doggy walks on the right side, carry the leash in your left hand. This may be slightly uncomfortable at first, but you'll see why it's required next.

Carry a handful of kibble or small treats in your pocket, the side your dog is on.

Every so often call your dog's name whilst holding a piece of kibble in your non leash hand.

Instruct your dog to walk behind your hand a few steps before rewarding him with the treat.

Gradually increase the time you call their name to the point you give them the treat. Keep repeating this every day for a few weeks.

Eventually your dog will come to recognize the good behavior of walking by your side may result in a tasty reward. Always care some treats with you to enforce the new walking style and preventing your pooch straying back into bad habits.

Dog Runs away or Gets Loose

You're walking your dog and suddenly the leash snaps or the collar slips, what do you do?

Contrary to popular belief, do not run after them. All doggy will do Is think it's a game of chase and just run faster.

Instead, lay down on the ground or pretend to be hurt. Your dog will think something is wrong and should come back to you to see if everything is okay.

That being said, this is no substitute for proper training. The best escape prevention is making sure everything is secure and your dog follows your commands.

Homemade Dog Sunscreen

What you need:

- 3 tbsp. sesame oil
- 2 tbsp. coconut
- 1 tbsp. natural beeswax
- ½ cup half& half
- 1 tsp. Calcium Montmorillonite Clay
- 3 tbsp. Pure Aloe Vera (no alcohol)
- 6 drops lavender essential oil
- 5 drops peppermint essential oil
- 2 drops carrot seed essential oil
- 2 drops myrrh essential oil
- 2 drops patchouli essential oil
- 1 drops helichrysum essential oil

Steps:

1. Mix sesame oil, coconut oil and wax. Broil until melted.
2. Remove from heat and mix in essential oils
3. In a bowl, mix tea brew, Aloe Vera, and clay together. Bring to lukewarm temperature in microwave

4. Whisk vigorously while slowly adding tea mixture into the oil mixture
5. Pour into a dark glass container and store in refrigerator
6. Apply as to exposed areas, reapply after swimming.
7. Wash off after done

Lost Dog

A lost dog can be a traumatic experience for both you and your pet. Following these tips can help you find your furry friend when all else seems hopeless.

Take an article of clothing from the dog owner that has been worn all day, the older the better, so the lost dog can pick up the scent. Leave the article of clothing at the spot where your dog was last seen and leave it there. You can also bring their crate or a familiar toy. Leave a note explaining the situation, requesting the clothing not be moved.

Also, leave a bowl of water as it is likely your dog hasn't drank in some time. Avoid leaving food as it can attract other animals.

Check back in a few hours or the next day. Hopefully your dog will be waiting there or nearby.

Bathing Tips

Having trouble with your pup in the tub? Here are two tips to ease your dog's cleaning time.

Use a tea pitcher or something similar to use for your dog's shampoo and rinsing them with water.

You can also use a shower cap to cover your dog's eyes and ears, to avoid shampoo running in their eyes and causing all sorts of problems.

Kong Fillers

The Kong, every dog's favorite toy!

There a hundreds of different recipes on the internet for countless days of tasty Kong filled goodness for your dog. Here are three of my favorite fillers for my furry friend.

1. Combine plain Cheerios or similar cereal and peanut butter in Kong and put in freezer for a few hours.
2. Combine a ripe banana, 2 big spoonfuls of peanut butters and a slice of cheese. Mix well and freeze with Kong for a few hours.
3. Combine a scrambled egg, meat, yogurt, cheese and mashed potatoes for a special occasion doggy omelet!

Finally, I'd like to thank you for taking the time to read this book. I hope you've enjoyed reading it as much as I did writing it.

Made in the USA
Middletown, DE
05 December 2019

80052639R00068